Growing kids
through diverse learning experiences™

Bur Bur & Friends™

Anna Goes Hiking

Discover Hiking and Explore Nature

By JoAnne Pastel & Kakie Fitzsimmons

Interface Publishing • Minneapolis

Copyright ©2007 by JoAnne Pastel and Kakie Fitzsimmons

All rights reserved. International copyright secured. No part of this book may be reproduced, stored in a retrieval system, or transmitted in any form or by any means—electronic, mechanical, photocopying, recording, or otherwise—without the prior written permission of Farmer's Hat Productions™, except for the inclusion of brief quotations in an acknowledged review.

Illustrations by Lindsay VanDeWeghe / www.ldutchdesign.com
Book design and art direction by Christopher Bohnet / www.xt4inc.com
Edited by Jodie Ahern with Judy Arginteanu
Project Manager Sarah Hermann

For more information on Bur Bur and Friends™ go to www.burburandfriends.com
or www.farmershatproductions.com

Interface Publishing
241 First Avenue North
Minneapolis, MN 55401 U.S.A.

Website address: www.interfacepublishing.com

Library of Congress Cataloging-in-Publication Data

Pastel, JoAnne.
  Anna goes hiking : discover hiking and explore nature / by JoAnne Pastel and Kakie Fitzsimmons.
     p. cm.
  ISBN-13: 978-0-9777121-7-5
  1. Hiking--Juvenile literature. 2. Nature trails--Juvenile literature. I. Fitzsimmons, Kakie. II. Title.
  GV199.52.P37 2007
  796.51--dc22
                                    2007022744

Manufactured in the United States of America
1 2 3 4 5 6 – DP – 12 11 10 09 08 07

To my little friend Anna.

— J. P.

In memory of my late uncles, Mike and Gerry,
who took me on my first hike at Madeline Island.

— K. F.

Anna and her family are planning their weekend. "Anna, would you like to go hiking?" asks Mom.

Hiking? What is hiking?

"Hiking is when you go on a long walk outside," replies Mom.

Yeah! Let's go!

Anna, Mom and Dad drive to the state park. Anna grabs her backpack, binoculars and walking stick.

I am ready to go hiking!

"That is a mama deer with two fawns," says Mom. "A baby deer is called a fawn. Do you see the white spots on their bodies? The spots help the fawns blend in with their surroundings to keep them safe in the forest."

Anna and Mom walk toward the deer, but the deer run away. Anna looks down and notices deer tracks on the path.

"Look at the different tracks the deer left on the path," says Mom.

That one is REALLY big, mama!

Anna turns and walks toward a pond.
She wonders what else they will find.

Look! A frog!

Dad turns to look, and the frog jumps off a lily pad floating in the water. The family stops to watch the frog as it swims away.

Ribbit, ribbit, you are a fast little froggy!

"Anna, do you want to keep hiking to see what else we can spot?" asks Mom.

Anna hears a loud *rat-a-tat-tat*. She looks up and sees a bird pecking at a tree.

Look at that bird!

"That is a woodpecker," says Dad. "Woodpeckers poke holes in trees with their beaks!"

"The woodpecker is searching for insects to eat," says Dad.

The woodpecker is red, white and black!

"Very good, Anna! You sure know your colors," says Mom.

Farther along the trail, Anna and her family notice a stream. In the stream is a pile of sticks and branches.

"Right over there," Dad says softly. "Do you see its brown body and flat tail?"

Yes! I see it!

A beautiful butterfly begins to dance to the birds' music. Anna pretends to play the flute as if she were a part of nature's band.

What stinks?

"That is a skunk smell," says Mom. "It is very stinky!"

"Skunks spray when they are afraid," says Dad. "This one probably heard us when we were talking about the ants."

"Now might be a good time to head back to our car," says Mom. "We can take a different trail to avoid the skunk smell."

What is that?

"It is a raccoon, Anna," replies Dad. "If you look closely, he seems to be wearing a mask."

That is silly, Dad!

As they get into their car, Anna sees a rabbit hopping.

Look, a rabbit!

"She is cute, Anna," says Mom. "I think she is going home, just like us."

"Anna, you are a good hiker!" says Mom. "What did you like the best about hiking today?"

It was fun being with you and Dad... and I liked seeing the ants, too!

Mom reads Anna a story and gives her a kiss.
"Good night, sleep tight, my little bunny!"

Good night, Mama.

Anna falls asleep and dreams about everything she saw on her hiking adventure.

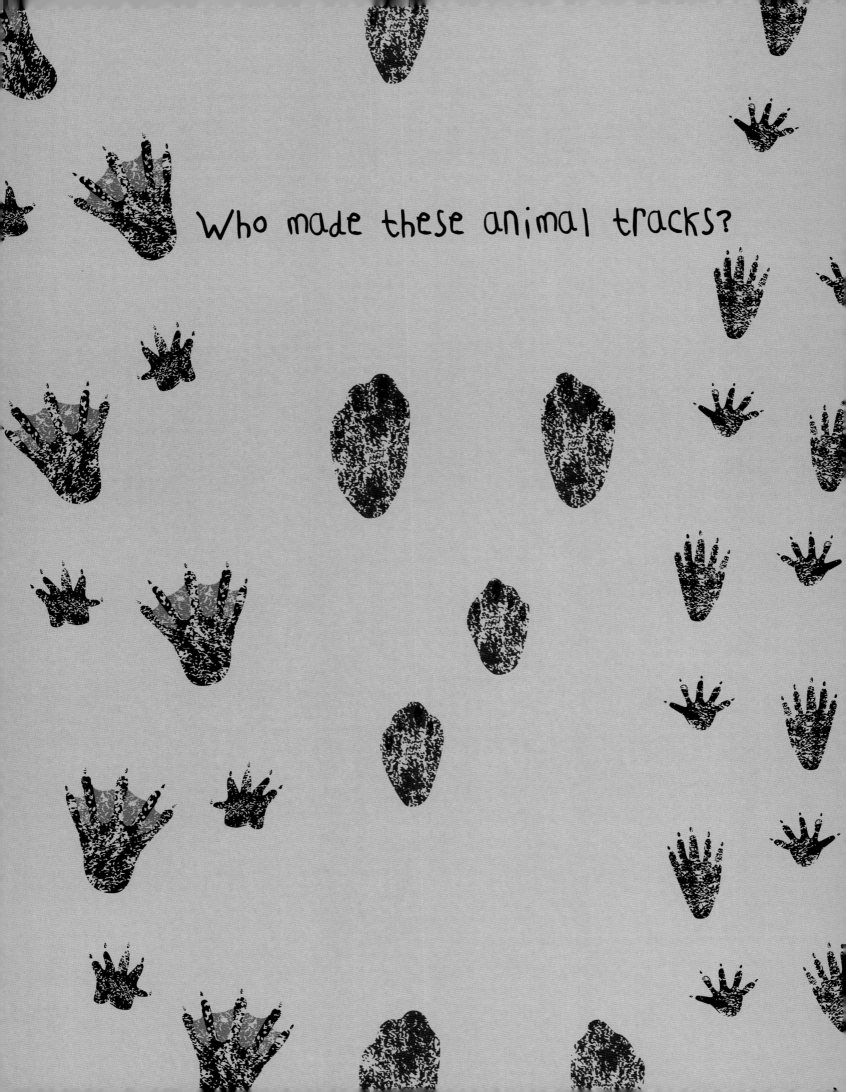

Look on the next page for help.

Beaver

- Large, flat tail helps the beaver swim
- Average weight is 31 to 60 pounds
- Eats bark, plants and small twigs
- Lives in dams, burrows or lodges made of branches and mud

Frog

- Eats bugs and worms
- Small amphibian with bulging eyes
- Lives in or near water
- Jumps on lily pads

Raccoon

- Bushy tail with 4 to 7 dark rings
- Eats insects, crayfish, fish, fruit, berries and nuts
- Lives near streams, lakes and marshes
- Baby raccoons are called kits

Striped Skunk

- Large feet and claws made for digging
- Eats mice, rats, roaches, yellowjackets, grubs, beetles, insects, fruit and nuts
- When threatened, will spray a smelly, oily fluid for protection
- Uses underground dens year-round for resting, hiding and giving birth

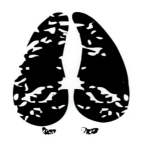

Deer

- Good swimmer and runner
- Eats green plants, nuts, trees, and twigs
- Lives in a small group called a herd
- Eyes are set wide apart

Pileated Woodpecker

- Grows from 6½ to 19 inches long
- Short legs, sharp-clawed toes and stiff tail
- Pecks on wood to search for food (insects) and to attract mates
- Eats carpenter ants, insects, beetle larvae, fruit and nuts

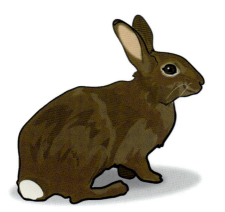

Cottontail Rabbit

- Long ears and long feet
- Moves very fast
- Eats grasses, fruits, vegetables and twigs
- Lives in a nest above ground

Ant

- Lives in a colony
- Eats crumbs, insects, nectar and honeydew melon
- Can carry 20 times its body weight
- Has six legs

Let's pack our backpack for the hike!

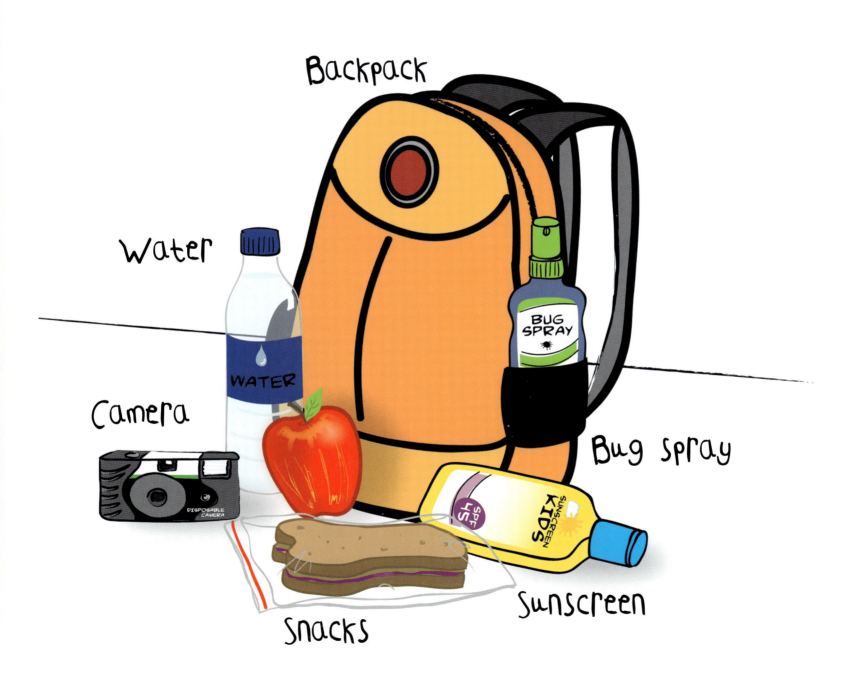